The Future We Face

James M. Vardaman

新たな未来に向かって —— 英語で考える私たちの世界

SANSHUSHA

Preface

The 15 chapters in this book deal with issues that our world faces today and will continue to face in the future. Each chapter is intended to encourage you to develop skills in thinking about the subject and increasing your vocabulary, so that you will be able to write your own ideas and talk about your views. The topics vary from education and welfare to tourism, science, and engineering.

Begin by reading the Introduction which will give you an overall view of the subject. The Vocabulary Building section will help you expand your use of various forms of words. You may know a noun or verb and discover the forms of adjectives and adverbs, too.

The Readings are approximately 250 words long. Read each one silently one time, then read it aloud several times, so you can discover the flow of the phrases. The Comprehension Check will help confirm whether you understood the reading correctly.

In the Listening Exercise, you will hear a man and a woman discussing the topic. Try to grasp each person's opinion. The following comprehension questions will help you check whether you really understood their conversation.

The final Writing Exercise is an opportunity for you to organize your own thoughts about the topic of the chapter. Write down your ideas. Then you can practice saying these ideas in the Speaking Exercise.

Through the active use of all four skills, you can develop your ability to communicate with people who do not speak Japanese. You can discuss important issues that we all face now and will need to cooperate in solving in the years to come.

Educate yourself, as much as possible.

James M. Vardaman

Contents

Unit 1

Building from Above

👆 Introduction

Until now the idea of building or constructing something has been based on gravity, so we have assumed that we need to start at the bottom and go up from there. However, with new technology, it has become possible to consider building things from above.

Vocabulary Building

Fill in the blanks by referring to the derivatives. If you are not sure, look it up in the dictionary.

Noun	Adjective	Verb	Adverb
a.	specific	b.	specifically
adjustment	adjustable	c.	
	basic		d.
e.	beneficial	benefit	beneficially

1. She didn't _____ when she would return to the office.

2. I'm trying to _____ myself to university life.

3. He's _____ a kind person.

Reading

 01

Wasps and bees are skillful flying builders. Working in teams, they deposit wax or wood pulp according to complex specifications that become hives or nests. They adjust their plans as they go, depending on the weather, materials, and available workers. Technology now is making it possible for humans using flying robots to do something similar. 5

Early 3D printers were limited by the range of the nozzle that deposited the material layer by layer. But scientists have developed drones which are basically two kinds of flying robots that can do the work of builders and supervisors. The builder robots carry the 3D-printing nozzle and the supervisor robots scan the progress of the builders. Layer by layer, these two types of robots deposit 10 material, make adjustments where necessary, and compute the next layer that is needed.

Flying robots have already proven capable of manufacturing small complex structures. As they become more advanced, they will be able to build large structures using different materials. Because they can operate almost anywhere, 15 they will be able to fix things in dangerous places or places that are not easy to get to. This might include cracks on tall buildings. They might be able to locate and seal leaks in pipelines carrying gas or oil in remote locations. An added benefit is that it would not be necessary to construct scaffolding to carry out construction. This alone would save considerable time and expense. Humans 20 will need new skills to make flying robots work right, but the benefits seem worth the effort.

(254 words)

Comprehension Check

1. T   F   Bees and wasps work independently in building hives.

2. T   F   3D printers place building materials one layer at a time.

3. T   F   New technology uses two types of robots to place material accurately.

4. T   F   In the future only small structure construction will be possible.

5. T   F   Flying robots may eventually be able to operate in remote areas.

///

Listening Exercise

Listen to the following conversation and answer the questions below.   02

1. Why is the man worried about robots building things?

    a. Because robots may make mistakes.

    b. Because robots may take people's jobs.

    c. Because robots are unsafe.

2. What is the woman's view about the human workers?

    a. They will continue to be necessary in the future.

    b. Their current skills will still be used.

    c. Workers will be monitored safely by robots.

Writing & Speaking Exercise

Organize your own ideas and write them down.

03

A: You know, it worries me just a little bit that there are technology and robots that are capable of building things so easily.

B: Why is that?

A: _____

_____

_____

_____

///

1. Listen to the start of the conversation above.

2. Now write a continuation of the conversation.

   • Brainstorm and put your ideas in the space below.

   [blank box]

   ─── You can use the tips below, if you need to. ───

   Possible ideas:

Strength of the building	Building materials are necessarily lighter.
Possible robot failure	A building built by a malfunctioning robot is unsafe.
Safety during construction	The drone might drop things by mistake.

   Start the conversation with this phrase:

   I am worried about ~ because ~
   I am concerned about ~.

   • Organize your own ideas and write them down in the underlined area above.

3. Practice the conversation using your model above.

Unit 2

Food Loss

☝ Introduction

Almost every country in the world is concerned about growing or otherwise obtaining enough food to feed its people. Some nations suffer constantly from severe weather conditions, lack of drinkable water, and famine. Other nations have more food than their people can consume. Food loss is an international issue.

Vocabulary Building

Fill in the blanks by referring to the derivatives. If you are not sure, look it up in the dictionary.

Noun	Adjective	Verb	Adverb
regularity	regular		**a.**
assumption		**b.**	
production, product	productive	**c.**	
consumer, consumption		**d.**	
necessity	necessary		**e.**

1. We _____ go to the supermarket, so we don't buy very much at one time.

2. I _____ that she would join us for lunch, so I prepared an extra portion.

3. You don't _____ have to attend the meeting.

Reading

 04

The media regularly tell us that global hunger is increasing. To eliminate—or at least reduce—hunger around the world, most people would assume that we have to produce more food. That's logical, but it may not be the only option. A partial solution may be to rethink what kind of food is grown, how that food is produced, and what happens to the food once it is available. 5

Efficient use of resources such as land is key to choosing the ideal kind of food that can be produced. In California, for example, valuable land is used to produce high-priced almonds. Profits from almonds may be appealing, but almonds are not an essential crop. The land could be used more efficiently in producing other crops. 10

A second inefficient agribusiness is the raising of cattle. Cows and pigs consume huge quantities of grain that could be directly eaten by humans. Diets with lots of meat may be tasty, but producing meat is expensive. It would be far better to use available agricultural land for grains like corn, beans, and wheat, for humans. 15

Once food is produced and packaged, it is not necessarily fully consumed. Foods like raw meat, fresh vegetables, and milk have a "best by" date. Portions of these food products end up as waste, which costs money to process. Many stores place discount prices on these items to encourage shoppers to purchase them. But there is still a lot left over. It's a real waste—and should be stopped. 20

(250 words)

Comprehension Check

1. **T F** Producing more food is the only way to reduce world hunger.

2. **T F** There are alternatives to increasing efficient ways of growing food.

3. **T F** Growing almonds is an uneconomical business.

4. **T F** Cattle are not consumers of the grains that humans eat.

5. **T F** Stores selling perishable foods have to throw away some items.

Listening Exercise

Listen to the following conversation and answer the questions below. 05

1. How has the man changed since he was younger?

   a. He has become a vegetarian.

   b. He has developed a diet that is healthier.

   c. He enjoys eating larger portions of everything.

2. What doesn't the woman suggest?

   a. We should eliminate meat from our diet.

   b. People should eat beans to get protein.

   c. Everyone should eat a healthier diet.

Writing & Speaking Exercise

Organize your own ideas and write them down. 06

A: Sometimes I have to throw out food because it has gone bad, but I feel bad about wasting it.

B: What do you think you could do to prevent that from happening?

A: _____

_____

_____

_____

//

1. Listen to the start of the conversation above.

2. Now write a continuation of the conversation.

   • Brainstorm and put your ideas in the space below.

You can use the tips below, if you need to.

Possible ideas:

Buy only what we need	We can check our refrigerator and pantry before shopping.
Know how to preserve food	If stored incorrectly, it can easily spoil.
Use leftovers in different ways	For example, you can make potato salad with *nikujaga*.

Start the conversation with this phrase:

To prevent food loss, we should ~.

We can ~ as a measure against food loss.

   • Organize your own ideas and write them down in the underlined area above.

3. Practice the conversation using your model above.

Unit 3

Identifying False Information

🖐 Introduction

When the internet and search engines first became available to almost everyone, it seemed much easier to find information. It didn't occur to a lot of people that the "information" might not be accurate or that it might even be dangerous. Learning what is accurate and what is inaccurate is now essential.

Vocabulary Building

Fill in the blanks by referring to the derivatives. If you are not sure, look it up in the dictionary.

Noun	Adjective	Verb	Adverb
a.	intelligent		intelligently
intent	**b.**	intend	intentionally
reliance	**c.**	rely	reliably
popularity	popular	**d.**	popularly
risk	**e.**	risk	
cruelty	**f.**		cruelly

1. He made a mistake, but it wasn't _____ so I forgave him.

2. So-called influencers try to _____ items on social media.

3. It seems _____ to me to climb a mountain without emergency equipment.

Reading

 07

When the internet and search engines like Google first came into wide use, it seemed like a dream come true. Anyone with a laptop or a smartphone could quickly find answers to almost any question. Now with artificial intelligence (AI) and ChatGPT, we have access to more information and even explanations of reasoning. But we should not forget that information may not always be 5 accurate.

We are now faced with learning how to detect and defend against misinformation, which is false or inaccurate. It is called disinformation when it is not simply false, but is intended to make people believe something that is not true. We can call it propaganda, especially if it is issued by a government or the 10 media.

Teaching children to detect misinformation is an essential part of media literacy, and teachers in Finland provide a good example. One method is to assign students to edit their own videos and photos, to show how easy it is to manipulate visual information. They have found edited videos on platforms that 15 completely change the background, people's faces, and the words they appear to say.

Another is to have students search words like "vaccination" and consider how search algorithms work. They discuss why the first results may not always be the most reliable. Top results may be popular because they are entertaining, 20 forceful, or promoted, but they may be completely inaccurate. If a viewer believes this "misinformation," it can lead to making decisions that are risky for health, misleading for politics, or cruel to certain individuals or groups.

(258 words)

Comprehension Check

1. T F Search engines make it possible to obtain lots of information.

2. T F What is not clear is whether the information is true or not.

3. T F Propaganda cannot be used to mislead people into believing lies.

4. T F Visual information can be modified to change images and speech.

5. T F The first result in an algorithm search is the most accurate one.

Listening Exercise

Listen to the following conversation and answer the questions below. 08

1. Why is the woman disappointed?

    a. Because the politician had bad policies.

    b. Because he lied about his past.

    c. Because he went to the wrong school.

2. What is the man's reaction?

    a. He doesn't believe that there will be more cases like that.

    b. He thinks that universities should be more careful.

    c. He believes trust through experience is important.

Writing & Speaking Exercise

Organize your own ideas and write them down. 09

A: There must be some way to find out whether data or information is accurate and dependable, isn't there?

B: I don't know. What do you suggest?

A: _____

_____

_____

_____

///

1. Listen to the start of the conversation above.

2. Now write a continuation of the conversation.

• Brainstorm and put your ideas in the space below.

```
┌─────────────────────────────────────────────────┐
│                                                 │
│                                                 │
│                                                 │
│                                                 │
│                                                 │
└─────────────────────────────────────────────────┘
```

You can use the tips below, if you need to.

Possible ideas:

Check the source of information	Government and corporate information may be reliable.
Check multiple sources of information	If multiple sources say the same thing, it's probably reliable.
Check the facts	It is possible that the facts and sources stated are false.

Start the conversation with this phrase:

I suggest that we should ~.
I recommend you to ~.

• Organize your own ideas and write them down in the underlined area above.

3. Practice the conversation using your model above.

Water Footprint

☝ Introduction

The goods and services we depend on in our daily lives have a "water footprint." Recognizing what that means can help us protect the environment and guide us to making good decisions about how we live. This is true for us as individuals as well as for every country.

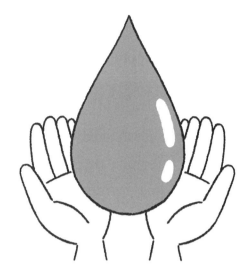

Vocabulary Building

Fill in the blanks by referring to the derivatives. If you are not sure, look it up in the dictionary.

Noun	Adjective	Verb	Adverb
creation, creativity	creative	**a.**	creatively
	distinguishable	**b.**	
pollution, **c.**	**d.**	pollute	
approximation	approximate	approximate	**e.**

1. I'm careful to _____ between real friends and "friends" on social media.

2. The water in the river is really _____ so no one should swim in it.

3. The station is _____ three kilometers from here.

Reading

The term "water footprint" describes the amount of water that is used to produce the goods and services we use. It can measure the water used in growing crops, producing a t-shirt, or creating gas for a car. It can also tell us how much water a country is using, from a river or an aquifer. The water footprint allows us to ask and answer a lot of questions, especially whether we 5 are protecting our water resources for the future of people and nature.

The water footprint distinguishes between green, blue, and grey water. Green water comes from rain and it is especially relevant for agriculture. Blue water is from surface or underground sources and it applies to industry and household uses. Grey water contains pollutants that end up in soil and lakes. These 10 measures are important in government policies, businesses, and communities.

In terms of the food that we consume, plant protein has a smaller footprint than animal protein. In the Netherlands, for example, a 150-gram soy burger has a footprint of about 160 liters of water. In comparison, a beef burger takes an average of 1,000 liters. 15

Looking at national scales, the water footprint of American citizens is 2,840 cubic meters per year per person. Approximately 20% of this is external, meaning from outside the country. Japan has a much lower footprint of 1,380 cubic meters per year per person. However, about 77% of the total water footprint is outside the borders of the country. Japan has lots of rain, but it imports an 20 enormous amount of goods from overseas.

(262 words)

Comprehension Check

1.   T   F   A "water footprint" can only be used in reference to farming.

2.   T   F   Several types of water are measured in each water footprint.

3.   T   F   These measurements can be of use to cities and governments.

4.   T   F   A water footprint can helpful in deciding what kind of foods we should produce.

5.   T   F   Water footprints measure only water that is used within one's own country.

///

Listening Exercise

Listen to the following conversation and answer the questions below. 11

1. What did the man become more aware of?

    a.   Where products are produced.

    b.   How much products cost.

    c.   Who has produced the goods.

2. How does the woman react to his comments?

    a.   She tells him he should be more conscious.

    b.   She is interested in where the goods come from.

    c.   She believes that what he says is significant.

Writing & Speaking Exercise

Organize your own ideas and write them down.

 12

A: I never knew anything about "water footprints" until now. It seems like an important measurement for ordinary people and for countries to consider.

B: In what ways could it affect us as individuals?

A: _____

_____

_____

_____

///

1. Listen to the start of the conversation above.

2. Now write a continuation of the conversation.

   • Brainstorm and put your ideas in the space below.

┌───┐
│   │
│   │
│   │
│   │
│   │
└───┘

You can use the tips below, if you need to.

Possible ideas:

Conserve water	Avoid leaving the water running when brushing your teeth
Choose domestic products	Check the origin of ingredients when shopping for food
Eat less beef	Try "meats" made from vegetables such as beans

Start the conversation with this phrase:

In my case, I try to ~.
Perhaps people will come to ~.

   • Organize your own ideas and write them down in the underlined area above.

3. Practice the conversation using your model above.

Unit 5

Data in Sports

👆 Introduction

Until the past decade, most professional athletes and sports fans have viewed numbers as a way of measuring achievement. In soccer, it is how many goals someone has scored. In baseball, it is a batting average, a pitching average, or homeruns scored. But now data is homework for every sport.

Vocabulary Building

Fill in the blanks by referring to the derivatives. If you are not sure, look it up in the dictionary.

Noun	Adjective	Verb	Adverb
value	**a.**	evaluate	
analysis, analyst, analytics	analytical	**b.**	
competition	**c.**	compete	
addition	**d.**	**e.**	additionally

1. _____ information will be necessary before we make a decision.

2. Critical thinking means having the ability to _____ an argument.

3. She is the most _____ player on the team.

Reading

Among the valuable participants in professional sport are superstar players and celebrated coaches. Recently, there is a third, highly sought figure: the data analyst.

Fans of sports such as soccer and baseball have long thought that it was natural skill, hard training, strong desire, and quick decision-making that made 5 an athlete a star. However, it has become clear that by carefully counting certain actions and studying their results, a player and a team can gain a competitive advantage.

Decades ago, "data" was collected by people with paper and pencil. It was processed by people adding figures and trying to understand what the totals 10 showed. Nowadays, video clips and computer analysis of data from games are much easier, but the analyst still has to interpret it. As a result, it is obvious that it is not just a player's physical preparation or performance that makes a difference. It is also a matter of which strategies work in specific situations.

In baseball, for instance, pitchers study what batters tend to do in different 15 situations. In reverse, batters do their homework on each pitcher they face the next day. In soccer (football) players study which side to attack from, which defender is easier to avoid, and how close to get before attempting a goal.

The use of analytics by more teams has had two effects. One is that data is used in deciding on new recruits. Another is that data analysis is no longer such 20 a great advantage; almost all elite teams are doing the same thing.

(254 words)

Comprehension Check

1. T F Data analysts have become valuable in pro sports.

2. T F Competitive advantages come only from hard training.

3. T F Methods for processing data have changed significantly.

4. T F Athletes carefully study what the other team's players do.

5. T F Not every professional team makes use of analytics.

//

Listening Exercise

Listen to the following conversation and answer the questions below.   14

1. Why is the woman surprised?

   a. She discovered that analytics were used in baseball games.

   b. She thought analytics were unnecessary in sports.

   c. She didn't know analytics were used in other sports.

2. What is true about data analytics in sports?

   a. It can be used by both sides in a competition.

   b. Analytics makes sports less interesting.

   c. Players no longer need to train as much.

Writing & Speaking Exercise

Organize your own ideas and write them down.

 15

A: What do you think it takes to make a strong team, in competitions like sports?

B: Well, I guess there are several things.

_____

_____

_____

_____

//

1. Listen to the start of the conversation above.

2. Now write a continuation of the conversation.

• Brainstorm and put your ideas in the space below.

:..:
:   :
:   :
:   :
:..:

---You can use the tips below, if you need to.---

Possible ideas:

Know the opposing team well   Strong points, weaknesses, team formations

Trust among members   Respect other team members, constant communication

Clarify goals   Know what you need to do, think positively

Start the conversation with this phrase:

First of all, it is important to ~.

~ is the best way to make a strong team.

• Organize your own ideas and write them down in the underlined area above.

3. Practice the conversation using your model above.

6 Community Kitchens

✌ Introduction

Usually when we say we are hungry, there is a way to get something to eat within a reasonable amount of time. Not everyone is so fortunate. There are people in almost every community, even in rich countries, who simply do not have enough money to feed themselves or their family.

Vocabulary Building

Fill in the blanks by referring to the derivatives. If you are not sure, look it up in the dictionary.

Noun	Adjective	Verb	Adverb
a.	**b.**		conveniently
donation		**c.**	
availability	**d.**		
collection	collectible, **e.**	collect	collectively

1. I'd like to come by and see you if Friday afternoon is _____.

2. Through our _____ efforts we won the final game.

3. Would you be _____ to discuss our project sometime soon?

Reading

Most of us take for granted being able to eat three meals a day. We can either shop and cook, drop in a fast-food shop, or stop by a convenience store. We manage to keep going without too much trouble.

But not everyone is fortunate to have even simple meals, and that is where several types of volunteer groups have stepped in. One variety is the "community 5 kitchen" where people in need can come to get a free hot meal at least once a day. Community centers and churches serve as drop-in sites where anyone can come and eat for free. This is a great service to homeless people and other people living below the poverty line. Ingredients may be donated by restaurants and even grocery stores. 10

Volunteers may also gather canned goods, packaged foods, and daily necessities for "food banks," where very poor families can pick them up. Volunteers may even deliver bags of goods to people who are unable to come pick them up.

A recent addition is the "community refrigerator." Participants can either 15 donate a refrigerator, donate money to purchase one, or pay for electricity. Someone may offer a place for it or offer to maintain it in good condition. Artists and builders can make the refrigerator attractive and protected from the weather. Others can bring items to put in the public refrigerator, which is available 24 hours a day. And anyone is free to take items from it or to provide 20 items. It is a collective effort that builds communities.

(254 words)

Comprehension Check

1. T F Getting something to eat is rather difficult for most people.

2. T F Community kitchens sell meals at reasonable prices.

3. T F Some places that serve free meals are in churches.

4. T F Food banks don't serve prepared meals to people.

5. T F There are many ways to contribute to community refrigerators.

//

Listening Exercise

Listen to the following conversation and answer the questions below.   17

1. Why do the grocery stores donate food products to the food bank?

   a. Because the time limit for product freshness is coming soon.

   b. Because the stores can benefit by giving food away.

   c. Because the products have just come out on the market.

2. What is the man thinking about doing?

   a. Volunteering to collect food for the community refrigerator.

   b. Offering money to support the community refrigerator.

   c. Helping gather food for the food bank.

Writing & Speaking Exercise

Organize your own ideas and write them down. 18

A: I've been thinking. I don't have a lot of time and sure don't have much money, but I wonder if there is some volunteer activity I could participate in.

B: What do you have in mind?

A: _____

_____

_____

_____

///

1. Listen to the start of the conversation above.

2. Now write a continuation of the conversation.

   • Brainstorm and put your ideas in the space below.

```
┌··········································································┐
:                                                                      :
:                                                                      :
:                                                                      :
:                                                                      :
:                                                                      :
:                                                                      :
:                                                                      :
└··········································································┘
```

───── You can use the tips below, if you need to. ─────

Possible ideas:

Online volunteer	No travel time or expense, easy to coordinate schedules
Community patrols	Walk pets when children are on their way to school
Learning to support children	Useful if you want to become a teacher

Start the conversation with this phrase:

I'm interested in ~

~ is what I want to do.

   • Organize your own ideas and write them down in the underlined area above.

3. Practice the conversation using your model above.

Unit 7

Studying Abroad

🖐 Introduction

In years past, many Japanese have hoped to go abroad to study, but nowadays fewer seem to be interested. Meanwhile larger numbers of foreign students—attracted by Japanese pop culture—have taken a serious interest in Japan and have come to study here. Studying abroad can benefit both people and countries.

Vocabulary Building

Fill in the blanks by referring to the derivatives. If you are not sure, look it up in the dictionary.

Noun	Adjective	Verb	Adverb
a.	attractive	b.	attractively
c.	encouraging	encourage	
admission		d.	
expansion	expansive	e.	

1. One of the main _____ for young visitors is Akihabara, where the latest electronic equipment and games are available.

2. Thanks to her words of _____ I was able to complete my project.

3. I must _____ that she is really sharp and comes up with very creative ideas.

Reading

 19

Whether they are first attracted to Japan by anime, manga, traditional culture, or unique foods, students from abroad have been eager to study in Japan. The opportunity to live for a year or so in Japan, get to know Japanese people, and experience local culture has great appeal.

In the short term, their curiosity and effort encourages the Japanese to 5 examine their own culture from different points of view. Japan also benefits in the long run, because these students often become bridge-builders between Japan and their home countries.

The reverse case is somewhat troubling. Until the 2000s, the number of Japanese seeking degrees overseas rose quickly and one-year study abroad 10 programs were quite popular. But by 2019 a government survey found that only a third of Japanese desire to study abroad. This compares with 51% of Germans and 66% of South Koreans.

Some public figures say that the decline is due to conservative employers who tend to avoid hiring students who have been abroad. Others explain that 15 it is the students' poor ability in foreign languages that prevents them from gaining admission to overseas schools. Still others say that the cost of studying abroad is too much of a strain on family budgets. All of these explanations may be accurate to some degree.

Japanese businesses, research institutes, and the government are 20 increasingly in need of innovative ideas, personal connections, and expanded networks of people and technology. If Japan is to regain some of its previous dynamism, it needs to encourage both students from abroad to come and Japanese students to venture abroad.

(262 words)

Comprehension Check

1. T F Few foreign students are attracted by the various cooked foods in Japan.

2. T F The fact that foreigners are interested in Japan stimulates Japanese, too.

3. T F Students who study abroad can later become cultural bridge-builders.

4. T F Fewer Germans than South Koreans want to study abroad.

5. T F Economic issues are not part of the reason few Japanese go abroad.

///

Listening Exercise

Listen to the following conversation and answer the questions below. 20

1. Why did the woman decide to apply to study in Japan?

   a. She was unable to study in Germany.

   b. Becoming interested in pop culture she wanted to learn about Japanese customs.

   c. She is planning to work for a company in Japan.

2. What is the man's reaction to her decision?

   a. He encourages her.

   b. He is unable to grasp her purpose.

   c. He plans to do the same.

Writing & Speaking Exercise

Organize your own ideas and write them down.

 21

A: I'm a little hesitant to say this, but I've been thinking about going abroad to study for a few months or maybe a year.

B: What are the pluses and minuses as you see them?

A: _____

_____

_____

_____

//

1. Listen to the start of the conversation above.

2. Now write a continuation of the conversation.

   • Brainstorm and put your ideas in the space below.

───────────── You can use the tips below, if you need to. ─────────────

Possible ideas:

Improve English skills   Helpful for employment and travel

Make friends abroad   Expand your horizons by spending time with foreign friends

Cost of studying abroad   Cost three million yen on average for one year

Start the conversation with this phrase:

The advantages/disadvantages of studying abroad for a few months/a year include ~.

~ is appealing, but I worry about ~

   • Organize your own ideas and write them down in the underlined area above.

3. Practice the conversation using your model above.

Unit 8

Enough Sleep

👆 Introduction

On average, Japanese sleep less than people in other countries. There are different views about why this is the case. Is it because appearing "hard-working" and "productive" is important? Whatever the case, lack of sleep is counter-productive and even harmful to health—and work habits.

Vocabulary Building

Fill in the blanks by referring to the derivatives. If you are not sure, look it up in the dictionary.

Noun	Adjective	Verb	Adverb
comparison	comparative	compare	**a.**
innovation, **b.**	innovative	innovate	
minimum	minimal	**c.**	minimally
diligence	**d.**		diligently
suggestion		**e.**	

1. Unfortunately, _____ few people get sufficient sleep on a routine basis.

2. Some of the most _____ workers accomplish a lot during remote work days.

3. I wouldn't _____ her contribution to the team's success.

Reading

International comparison surveys regularly show that on average Japanese simply do not sleep enough. In fact, Japan has one of the lowest national average sleep hours in the entire world. As an example of the gap, consider the following average sleep hours: New Zealand 7 hours 40 minutes, England 7 hours 33 minutes, America 7 hours 19 minutes, and Japan 6 hours 18 minutes. 5 Perhaps that is the reason why Japan has so many coffee shops and explains why Japan was the innovator of the canned coffee in its vending machines.

World-famous entrepreneurs often boast about needing only four or five hours of sleep per night and still being highly creative during the day. But that doesn't work for everyone. In fact, the reverse is probably true. 10

Perhaps this short-sleep habit begins when preparation for college entrance exams minimizes sleep. It may continue as workers convince themselves that long working hours show diligence. Less time in bed means more time for activities considered "productive"—whether it is work, study, or leisure activities. 15

Insufficient sleep, however, affects sustained attention during the daytime. One doesn't have to be a commercial pilot or an automobile driver to know that even a brief two-second gap in attention can lead to accidents. Students who fall asleep in class and employees who fall asleep in meetings may not be endangering lives, but their performance certainly declines. 20

So-called "revenge sleeping" on the weekends is aimed at "catching up" on sleep, but research suggests that it is not possible to sleep ten hours on the weekends and feel refreshed on Monday morning.

(264 words)

Comprehension Check

1. T   F   On average, people in New Zealand sleep an hour or so more than the Japanese.

2. T   F   Getting less sleep means you can be more productive during the day.

3. T   F   Sustained attention is basically unrelated with the number of hours slept.

4. T   F   Diligence cannot be measured by the number of hours one sleeps.

5. T   F   Sleeping longer on weekends is a successful strategy for becoming refreshed.

///

Listening Exercise

Listen to the following conversation and answer the questions below.   23

1. Why does the man ask her about the time she goes to sleep and gets up?

    a. He wonders whether lack of sleep affects her concentration.

    b. He thinks she is working too hard at night.

    c. He is rude in asking her a personal question.

2. How does the woman justify her late hours in the evening?

    a. She doesn't return home until late in the evening.

    b. Her friends are keeping the same hours that she does.

    c. She is busy and forgets what time it is.

Writing & Speaking Exercise

Organize your own ideas and write them down.

A: Foreign visitors regularly comment on how surprised they are that so many Japanese sleep on trains.

B: Why do they do that? Isn't that normal everywhere?

A: _____

_____

_____

_____

//

1. Listen to the start of the conversation above.

2. Now write a continuation of the conversation.

   • Brainstorm and put your ideas in the space below.

You can use the tips below, if you need to.

Possible ideas:

Don't worry about theft or molestation	Rare in Japan's public places
Don't oversleep	Seems like a special talent
Being quiet	Normal in foreign countries to chat on trains

Start the conversation with this phrase:

I heard that they are surprised that Japanese people ~.
They seem surprised that the Japanese ~.

   • Organize your own ideas and write them down in the underlined area above.

3. Practice the conversation using your model above.

Drones to the Rescue

☞ Introduction

Drones have already proven to be useful in obtaining beautiful visuals, rescuing people in trouble, and easing the burden on farmers. Further advances in the use of drones are likely to result from the development of drones that can operate accurately far beyond the sight of the operator.

Vocabulary Building

Fill in the blanks by referring to the derivatives. If you are not sure, look it up in the dictionary.

Noun	Adjective	Verb	Adverb
irrigation	irrigated	**a.**	
limit, limitation	limited	**b.**	
stability	stable	**c.**	
dependence, dependency	**d.** dependent	depend	dependably
transportation		**e.**	

1. She is highly _____ so you can count on her to do what she promises.

2. Government policies are sometimes necessary to _____ the prices of essentials.

3. My chances of buying a car are _____ because I haven't saved much money.

Reading

We live in an age in which drones carrying cameras provide us with a view of magnificent mountaintops, winding rivers, and crowded city streets. Drones patrol streets, monitor rooftops, and help find people who are lost. They can also patrol high-crime areas to protect local residents. Farmers use them to check irrigated fields and spot sections that need pesticides or additional nutrients. 5

Despite some problems and occasional accidents, the use of drones seems unlimited. If there is one downside to these devices today, it is the limitation of visual-line-of-sight control. In a large percentage of cases, the operator who controls the drone has to keep the drone within sight. This obviously limits its range. 10

The key to the future of drone usage will be remote control, in other words beyond line-of-sight operation, and eventually independent operation. Both of these will require stable GPS access, which is not always possible, especially in mountainous areas or areas with dense forests.

If long-distance use becomes dependable, drones can be put to many uses. 15 One example that is already in operation in Africa is long-distance delivery of medicine to villages which are completely cut off from hospital access. These are areas where the roads are impassable due to weather and local political conflicts. Carefully packaged medical supplies can be transported by a drone and dropped at a preset location. The drone can then return to its original base. 20 This is an excellent example of what drones could do to help people in need. And there will be even more uses in the future.

(259 words)

Comprehension Check

1. **T F** Drones can be employed to locate people who are lost.

2. **T F** Drones are of little use in urban areas.

3. **T F** Until now the distance between operators and drones has been limited.

4. **T F** Delivery of medicine to distant locations is not yet possible.

5. **T F** Drones can be programmed to make a delivery and then return.

//

Listening Exercise

Listen to the following conversation and answer the questions below. 26

1. What is the man's opinion about some uses of drones?

   a. He believes that drones are more dangerous than beneficial.

   b. He recognizes that there are many beneficial uses of drones.

   c. He anticipates that drones will be of limited use in the future.

2. What does the woman think about drone usage?

   a. She thinks that they may be of use to various types of people.

   b. She is worried about the dangers that drones present to society.

   c. She is not optimistic about the future use of drones in society.

Writing & Speaking Exercise

Organize your own ideas and write them down.

 27

A: It seems clear that drones are part of our future. I wonder whether they will be primarily beneficial to society or just the opposite.

B: Well, what do you think are the positives and negatives?

A: _____

_____

_____

_____

/ /

1. Listen to the start of the conversation above.

2. Now write a continuation of the conversation.

   • Brainstorm and put your ideas in the space below.

--------You can use the tips below, if you need to.--------

Possible ideas:

Access to places where people can't easily go	For example, underpopulated areas, mountains
Resolving labor shortages in logistics	Low shipping costs
Risk of accidents	Damage or loss of goods

Start the conversation with this phrase:

On the positive/negative side, ~

Advantages/disadvantages of using drones include ~

   • Organize your own ideas and write them down in the underlined area above.

3. Practice the conversation using your model above.

Country Mouse or City Mouse?

🖐 Introduction

Each of us has a preference for the type of work we do and the type of place we want to live in. As times change and as we grow older, we may decide that our current situation is no longer appealing. If there are other options, we may seriously begin to consider making changes.

Vocabulary Building

Fill in the blanks by referring to the derivatives. If you are not sure, look it up in the dictionary.

Noun	Adjective	Verb	Adverb
employee, a. , b.	employed	employ	
appeal	appealing	c.	
elimination		d.	
subsidy		e.	

1. Roger says that his _____ is always complaining about his work habits.

2. Living in the city _____ to most young people.

3. My favorite soccer team was _____ in the semi-finals, so I was disappointed.

Reading

28

Previously, it was common for young people to leave rural districts and look for employment in the cities. Once they left, they tended not to return. The countryside offered little in the way of jobs and the future of farming wasn't particularly appealing. Metropolitan populations grew and rural populations dropped.   5

But as the cities have grown crowded and rents have gone up, some younger singles and even families have been looking for a change of pace. Looking for a more appealing work-life balance, eliminating long commutes on crowded trains, and having more living space, they don't mind giving up the so-called advantages of the city.   10

Online nomads can work anywhere as long as they have stable internet connections. Home delivery services enable them to order electronic equipment, office supplies, and other essentials, so they don't even need a car for transportation. Some of these new residents happily leave behind desk jobs and long hours to take up farming with the help of cooperative local residents.   15

Enabling these would-be migrants are various NGOs in rural areas where depopulation is a problem. New residents give new life to communities with new skills. Some are interested in learning the new skills themselves, including basic farming skills and even forestry. Some local governments subsidize housing and child care for newcomers.   20

With patience and a show of respect on both sides, the immigrants from the city can benefit from their kind neighbors and the long-term residents can benefit from new, younger neighbors. Both sides can clearly gain from the expansion of these local communities.

(259 words)

Comprehension Check

1. **T F** In the past, most young people looked for work in the rural areas.

2. **T F** One problem in the cities is maintaining a work-life balance.

3. **T F** Most new residents in the country miss the excitement of the city.

4. **T F** New rural residents may also change the work they do.

5. **T F** Local communities may actually benefit from the new immigrants.

//

Listening Exercise

Listen to the following conversation and answer the questions below.   29

1. What did the woman want to do when she was in high school?

   a. She wanted to go live in a place that was exciting.

   b. She missed some things that she had at home in the country.

   c. She didn't want to do the same things as most young people.

2. What feelings do the two people share?

   a. A fear of starting a new life in a new city.

   b. A desire to return to life in the country.

   c. Difficulty in finding people to do things with.

Writing & Speaking Exercise

Organize your own ideas and write them down.   🎧 30

A: I have to admit, I worried about adjusting to life in college.

B: Why is that?

A: _____

_____

_____

_____

//

1. Listen to the start of the conversation above.

2. Now write a continuation of the conversation.

   • Brainstorm and put your ideas in the space below.

```



```

┌─── **You can use the tips below, if you need to.** ───┐

Possible ideas:

Transportation connections	Taking a train in the wrong destination
Crowded trains	Not being used to crowds
Driving a car	Being an inexperienced driver

Start the conversation with this phrase:

I'm from the countryside/city, so I wasn't good at ~
I worried about ~ because ~

   • Organize your own ideas and write them down in the underlined area above.

3. Practice the conversation using your model above.

Unit 11

Digital vs. Paper

☝ Introduction

Within a short period, we have shifted from a paper-based world to one that is based on screens and monitors. Digital access to information in many ways seems more convenient and accessible, but this shift away from printed paper may have changed the way we learn and the way we act.

Vocabulary Building

Fill in the blanks by referring to the derivatives. If you are not sure, look it up in the dictionary.

Noun	Adjective	Verb	Adverb
a.		tend	
consequence	**b.**		consequentially
stimulation	**c.**	stimulate	
length	**d.**		
	significant		**e.**

1. The way he behaved that afternoon changed my opinion of him
   _____.

2. Her presentation was quite _____ and I came away greatly impressed.

3. There is an occasional _____ among young people to take unnecessary risks.

Reading

 31

If the older generation tends to depend on analog technology, the younger generations seem more comfortable with a digital mindset. The transition from the former to the latter is now considered essential in business, government, and research. Yet some experts still defend the use of an ancient technology: paper. 5

One reason for this is that something written or printed on paper tends to be seen as more consequential. The same content presented on a screen may be seen as short-lived and quickly forgettable. One example is a study that found that paper calendars stimulated different behaviors from digital calendars. The users of old-fashioned ones made more detailed project plans than those 10 looking at an app. Furthermore, they were more likely to stick to the plans they made. Seeing lots of days at once on paper calendars makes a difference.

When it comes to lengthy reading, a portable e-book platform certainly has its merits, but is the reader's comprehension and memory the same in both cases? One research project found that customers place greater value on the 15 physical version of a product than one in a digital form. Shoppers are more willing to pay more for books they can hold in their hand than simply download.

Consider the difference between a letter and an email. Which would you pay more attention to? If it were a personal letter, then the former would be more significant and you would read it more carefully. 20

(241 words)

Comprehension Check

1. T F There is a gradual change away from an analog mindset.

2. T F The need for paper has been completely eliminated.

3. T F Content presented on paper may not seem as significant as that on an app.

4. T F Planning via digital apps is far more effective than using paper.

5. T F Most people would value a printed letter more than an email.

///

Listening Exercise

Listen to the following conversation and answer the questions below. 32

1. Why doesn't the woman want all government information to come digitally?

    a. It's harder for her to read websites and email.

    b. Digital communication is more expensive to use.

    c. She doesn't use a laptop or a smartphone.

2. How does the man react to her opinion?

    a. He completely disagrees with her.

    b. He thinks printed communication is superior.

    c. He disagrees with some parts and agrees with others.

Writing & Speaking Exercise

Organize your own ideas and write them down.

 33

A: There is so much information floating around that I don't have time to keep up with everything. It's hard to know what is important and what is even true.

B: What do you mean by that?

A: _____

_____

_____

_____

//

1. Listen to the start of the conversation above.

2. Now write a continuation of the conversation.

• Brainstorm and put your ideas in the space below.

```
```

You can use the tips below, if you need to.

Possible ideas:

Social media	Being inclined to believe information spread by friends
Online news	Sensational, but sometimes misinformed
E-mail	Includes junk mail as well as email with necessary information

Start the conversation with this phrase:

Take ~ for example.
To show you what I mean, ~

• Organize your own ideas and write them down in the underlined area above.

3. Practice the conversation using your model above.

Where Does Nuclear Waste Go?

🖐 Introduction

In discussions of nuclear power, not much attention is given to where to put nuclear waste. If we want to use energy created by nuclear power plants, we need to plan ahead about how to deal with the waste, not just for the short term, but for the long term, too.

Vocabulary Building

Fill in the blanks by referring to the derivatives. If you are not sure, look it up in the dictionary.

Noun	Adjective	Verb	Adverb
construction	a.	b.	constructively
impression	c.	impress	impressively
d.		locate	
e. , store		store	

1. There is a very large difference between just complaining and _____ criticism.

2. The presentation was quite _____ and the committee approved the project.

3. A good _____ is essential if a store wants to draw in customers.

Reading

Although solar, wind, thermal, and wave power are appealing alternatives to fossil fuels like natural gas, coal, and petroleum, they currently provide only small percentages of our power. It is not surprising, therefore, that some governments find nuclear power to be an attractive source of energy. However, a major downside of nuclear power is the waste that it creates. What can you do ⁵ with dangerous nuclear waste?

Finland is in the lead in dealing with such waste. The country is constructing a facility called Onkalo—the Finnish word for "cavity" or "pit." When it is completed, it will be the world's first permanent disposal site for high-level nuclear waste. High-level waste is extremely dangerous, and by "permanent," ¹⁰ the Finns mean 100,000 years.

This impressive project provides hope for the future of nuclear power, after hopes for expanding nuclear power were reduced by the disasters at Chernobyl and Fukushima Daiichi.

Because it is a land of volcanoes, frequent earthquakes, and occasional ¹⁵ tsunamis, Japan has no place to put its waste. The nuclear waste that has gathered at the Fukushima Daiichi site is kept in "temporary storage." There is little hope of locating a permanent storage site for any of this waste. Releasing any of the contaminated water into the Pacific Ocean is undesirable on the part of nearby residents, local fishermen, and people in other Asian nations. ²⁰

If Japan is unable to find a dependable way of storing nuclear waste permanently, is it reasonable to continue creating more nuclear waste?

(249 words)

Comprehension Check

1. T F Nuclear power does not appeal to national governments.

2. T F The Finnish project can be used for non-nuclear waste.

3. T F Onkalo will be a temporary storage site.

4. T F It is not likely that Japan can create a permanent waste storage.

5. T F Japanese are not worried about the release of contaminated water.

//

Listening Exercise

Listen to the following conversation and answer the questions below.   35

1. What does the woman say about fossil fuels?

    a. There is a large supply of them in different locations.

    b. Fossil fuels are a source of air pollution.

    c. They are a good source of power for residential needs.

2. What does the man bring up as a potential issue?

    a. Nuclear power is not sufficient for industrial needs.

    b. Residential needs cannot be met by fossil fuel sources.

    c. Not everyone wants to live near a nuclear power plant.

Writing & Speaking Exercise

Organize your own ideas and write them down.

 36

A: Nuclear power plants provide jobs to local people and produce power we need, but there is a problem of what to do with the nuclear waste.

B: What do you think is a possible solution?

A: _____

_____

_____

_____

//

1. Listen to the start of the conversation above.

2. Now write a continuation of the conversation.

   • Brainstorm and put your ideas in the space below.

You can use the tips below, if you need to.

Possible ideas:

Cooperation among nations	Combine knowledge and technology
Renewable energy sources	Solar/wind/geothermal/hydroelectric/biomass energy
Development of new technologies	Invent more energy-efficient machines and systems

Start the conversation with this phrase:

We can solve that problem by ~

To deal with that problem, I think ~ is helpful.

   • Organize your own ideas and write them down in the underlined area above.

3. Practice the conversation using your model above.

Farms without Fields

☞ Introduction

The traditional farm depends on a large amount of available land and water. It depends on chemicals to help crops grow and to prevent insects and plant diseases. It is also vulnerable to temperature changes and weather damage. A new type of farming offers a solution to multiple problems, in new locations.

Vocabulary Building

Fill in the blanks by referring to the derivatives. If you are not sure, look it up in the dictionary.

Noun	Adjective	Verb	Adverb
agriculture	**a.**		
b.		cultivate	
rotation		**c.**	
alternative	alternative	**d.**	alternately
growth		**e.**	

1. Local farmers are experimenting with the _____ of new types of rice.

2. Some countries have a limited amount of _____ land.

3. At our house, we _____ between cooking dinner at home and eating out.

Reading

 37

A new type of farmer has no fields, no agricultural machinery, and no worries about changes in the weather. These farmers have no soil and no need for sunshine. These new farmers may be the beginning of a revolution.

The "farm" where Dan Albert, who lives in cloudy, rainy Seattle, grows his crops is in his garage. He cultivates small green vegetables like radishes and 5 arugula. They grow in vertically stacked trays that slowly rotate. In the limited space in his garage, he grows them with hydroponics, a method that enables the plants' roots to sit in water filled with nutrients, instead of in soil. And in place of sunlight, he depends on LED lighting. Within two weeks, his crops go from seeds to harvest and go directly to restaurants, farmers' markets, and local groceries. 10

This alternative to soil-based farming is also being used on a larger scale in empty warehouses and disused factories as a new way to produce food. Large-scale "vertical farms" use control software to pump regular amounts of water and nutrients to the crops and to control lighting. By using power in the off-peak hours at night, electricity rates are lower. 15

Because crops are grown inside a building instead of in an open field, there is less need for pesticides and chemicals that kill weeds. Other major advantages are avoiding weather damage and extremes in temperature. Software can handle the daily care of the crops. The farmer can check his "farms" remotely, adjust the water supply, and change the lighting. All that can be done with a 20 simple smartphone.

(263 words)

Comprehension Check

1. T F The new farmers find fields and soil to be inessential.

2. T F Hydroponics is a method that adds nutrients to soil using water.

3. T F The new method cultivates crops inside buildings.

4. T F Vertical farms can be operated with lower-cost electricity.

5. T F Extreme weather and temperature changes cease to be issues.

//

Listening Exercise

Listen to the following conversation and answer the questions below.   38

1. What is the woman's initial comment about vertical farms?

   a. She is very doubtful about their success.

   b. She thinks they are a brilliant idea.

   c. She doesn't seem to know much about them.

2. What is the man's reaction to the idea?

   a. He shares her enthusiasm about the method.

   b. He is worried about the source of electric power.

   c. He has a different opinion regarding the vertical farms.

Writing & Speaking Exercise

Organize your own ideas and write them down.

 39

A: Considering that Japan's food self-sufficiency is only 38%, it seems to me that Japan might consider vertical farming.

B: What do you mean?

A: _____

_____

_____

_____

//

1. Listen to the start of the conversation above.

2. Now write a continuation of the conversation.

• Brainstorm and put your ideas in the space below.

```
┌──────────────────────────────────────────────────┐
│                                                    │
│                                                    │
│                                                    │
│                                                    │
│                                                    │
│                                                    │
└──────────────────────────────────────────────────┘
```

────────── You can use the tips below, if you need to. ──────────

Possible ideas:

Shrinking population involved in agriculture	Easy to manage production
Dependence on imports	Support for domestic producers
Poor crops	Not easily affected by weather conditions

Start the conversation with this phrase:

I mean, vertical farming can deal with ~
Well, vertical farming can handle ~.

• Organize your own ideas and write them down in the underlined area above.

3. Practice the conversation using your model above.

Unit 14

School Starting Age

Introduction

In most countries, the age at which children begin elementary school is determined by law. Parents are usually eager for their children to begin school as soon as possible. However, in America now, some parents and teachers are rethinking this, and they see a surprising benefit in delaying entrance.

Vocabulary Building

Fill in the blanks by referring to the derivatives. If you are not sure, look it up in the dictionary.

Noun	Adjective	Verb	Adverb
advantage	a.		
maturity	mature	b.	
prosperity	c.	d.	
impulse	e.		impulsively

1. In learning English it is _____ to have friends who are native speakers.

2. _____ action can be risky, so think carefully first.

3. Using new technology, the two friends developed a _____ business.

Reading

At first glance, it seems logical that starting school early gives a child an advantage. The child begins mastering skills as early as possible. But in America and other developed countries, some educators and parents are questioning that idea. They suggest holding the boys back one year, to give them more time to mature before beginning school. 5

Neuroscience research shows that in brain development there is a different course for boys and girls. When boys and girls start at the same age, the boys fail to keep up with their female classmates. The gap is mostly driven by social and emotional factors, not academic ones, and it continues.

Giving boys an extra boost may sound odd, especially considering the 10 inequities that many girls and women still face. But in education, boys and men need more help. When schools fail boys, those boys grow into men who lack the skills necessary to prosper in the workplace. They lack the skills to be strong partners and to be good providers for their families.

Pilot programs that are holding boys back one year show that hyperactivity 15 and inability to concentrate in boys is reduced. Among teenagers, these boys show more impulse control, ability to plan, and desire to avoid risk for short-term rewards.

Giving boys one extra year in kindergarten and pre-school before starting first grade could ensure that boys benefit from primary and secondary education, 20 go on to college, and have better job opportunities. The benefits for their future wives and children may well be quite significant.

(255 words)

Comprehension Check

1. T F Some American parents want to delay their son's school entrance.

2. T F Difference in brain development is not proven by science.

3. T F There is an academic gap between boys and girls.

4. T F Giving boys an extra boost is unfair to girls.

5. T F The benefits of holding boys back would be enjoyed not only by boys.

//

Listening Exercise

Listen to the following conversation and answer the questions below.   41

1. What did the man feel like in his early school years?

    a. He always felt confident and capable.

    b. He felt just as mature as the boys.

    c. He felt less mature than the girls.

2. What does the woman say about the option of holding boys back one year?

    a. She explains what some scientists and parents are thinking.

    b. She disagrees with the idea of giving boys an extra year to grow up.

    c. She believes that giving boys an extra year is wise.

Writing & Speaking Exercise

Organize your own ideas and write them down.

 42

A: When I look back at my own childhood, it never occurred to me that boys might mature slower than girls.

B: Do you think it would be a good idea to delay school entrance for boys for one year?

A: _____

_____

_____

_____

///

1. Listen to the start of the conversation above.

2. Now write a continuation of the conversation.

• Brainstorm and put your ideas in the space below.

⎡⎺⎺⎺⎺⎺⎺⎺⎺⎺⎺⎺⎺⎺⎺⎺⎺⎺⎺⎺⎺⎺⎺⎺⎺⎺⎺⎺⎺⎺⎤

⎣_____⎦

You can use the tips below, if you need to.

Possible ideas:

Easy to handle	Students are at about the same level
Depends on the personality	Would hinder the mature boys
How to spend the year delaying	Concern about working parents returning to work

Start the conversation with this phrase:

I agree/disagree with that idea.

I'm sure this idea is good. / I'm not sure this idea is good.

• Organize your own ideas and write them down in the underlined area above.

3. Practice the conversation using your model above.

Unit 15

The Appeal of Japan's Pop Culture

☞ Introduction

Decades ago Japanese industry was a world leader in many ways. Today the tourists who come to Japan are less interested in business than in culture. What appeals to them is not limited to what is newest but also includes some of the oldest cultural traditions of the country.

Vocabulary Building

Fill in the blanks by referring to the derivatives. If you are not sure, look it up in the dictionary.

Noun	Adjective	Verb	Adverb
economy	economic	**a.**	economically
resident	**b.**	reside	
promotion	promotional	**c.**	
inevitability	**d.**		**e.**

1. Based on my experience, it is _____ that prices will continue to rise.

2. If we _____ now maybe we can save enough money to travel abroad.

3. I'm on a tight budget so I have to choose an inexpensive _____ area to live in.

Reading

Japan was once famous as an economic superpower, as portrayed in the best-seller "Japan as Number One." The economy boomed with the export of top-class electronic goods and well-built automobiles. Foreign businesspeople came to study Japan's production methods.

In recent decades, however, the country has become more internationally 5 known for its "soft power." Anime, manga, cosplay, J-pop, street fashion, and "cuteness" have turned Japan into a destination for tourists from around the world.

The national government began promoting "Cool Japan" as a slogan to encourage cultural exports as well as inbound tourism. The public broadcaster 10 NHK developed a long-running television series called "Cool Japan." In it foreign residents of Japan from different countries commented on Japanese customs, events, and creations.

Large numbers of tourists visit Akihabara to find the most updated gaming systems and Harajuku to discover the most recent fashions. They may already 15 know which shops to visit, thanks to social media influencers. But they inevitably find something that they didn't know about. Things change day by day in the world of "Cool Japan."

In addition to searching out what is most up-to-date, most visitors from abroad are still going to the traditional sites like Sensoji Temple and the Meiji 20 Shrine in Tokyo and Kiyomizu Temple and Nijo Castle in Kyoto. Some visitors focus on kitchen implements in Kappabashi, traditional pottery in northern Kyushu, and hand-woven material in Kyoto. It is not just the "cool" parts of Japan that draw tourists. Japan has many reasons to make a long stay very attractive.

(253 words)

Comprehension Check

1. **T** **F** Japan's days as an economic superpower are in the past.

2. **T** **F** Tourists from overseas are only interested in new things.

3. **T** **F** The "Cool Japan" program features tourists from other countries.

4. **T** **F** Social media have contributed to the effort to draw tourists.

5. **T** **F** Travelers who come are also attracted to traditional Japanese things.

//

Listening Exercise

Listen to the following conversation and answer the questions below.   44

1. How was the woman influenced by her father's interest in literature?

   a. She wasn't particularly attracted to it.

   b. She found it to be quite unique.

   c. She was stimulated by what she read.

2. How did her interest in Japan develop?

   a. It started with a family trip to Japan.

   b. She found a "study abroad" program at her university.

   c. It developed step by step to an interest in customs and history.

Writing & Speaking Exercise

Organize your own ideas and write them down.

45

A: I've been thinking about studying in Japan during my university years, maybe for a year or just during summer break. Please recommend where I should go and what to do in Japan.

B: _____

_____

_____

_____

///

1. Listen to the start of the conversation above.

2. Now write a continuation of the conversation.

   • Brainstorm and put your ideas in the space below.

---You can use the tips below, if you need to.---

Possible ideas:

Kyoto	Traditional Japanese culture and crafts
Hiroshima	Peace
Gumma	Hot springs

Start the conversation with this phrase:

I recommend that you ~

~ is a great place to ~

   • Organize your own ideas and write them down in the underlined area above.

3. Practice the conversation using your model above.

著　者
James M. Vardaman（ジェームス・バーダマン）

新たな未来に向かって
英語で考える私たちの世界

2024 年 2 月 20 日　　第 1 版発行

著　者　　James M. Vardaman
発行者　　前田俊秀
発行所　　株式会社　三修社
　　　　　〒 150-0001 東京都渋谷区神宮前 2-2-22
　　　　　TEL 03-3405-4511　　FAX 03-3405-4522
　　　　　振替 00190-9-72758
　　　　　https://www.sanshusha.co.jp
　　　　　編集担当 伊藤宏実・三井るり子
印刷・製本　日経印刷株式会社

©2024 Printed in Japan ISBN978-4-384-33533-0 C1082
表紙デザイン―NON Design
本文デザイン & DTP―Shibasaki Rie
本文イラスト―田原直子
準拠音声制作―高速録音株式会社
　　　　　　　（吹込：Howard Colefield / Jennifer Okano）

教科書準拠 CD 発売
本書の準拠 CD をご希望の方は弊社までお問い合わせください。